Norooz

A Celebration of Spring!
The Persian New Year

Written by Gail Hejazi
Illustrated by Christina Cavallo

Dedication:
To everyone around the world, sharing commonality through celebration!
And to my children, Ava and Arshan, for whom I wrote this, that they may
share their heritage with others.
G.H.

In Gratitude:
To my husband, Shahram, and my in-laws for sharing their wonderful,
delicious culture with me. To Chrissy, for her artistry, generosity, and
belief in this book. To Beth, Brittany, Naseem and Shazzy for editing
assistance. To my family for their loving support and belief in me.
G.H.

Pronunciation Guide

Norooz - no-rooz

Iran - ee-ron

Chahar Shanbeh Soori - cha-har shan-beh sue-ree

Sorkhi-e toe az man, zardi-e man az toe - sor-khee-eh toe az
   man, zar-dee -eh man az toe

Qashohg-zany - ghosh-ogh zah-nee

Haji Firouz - ha-jee fee-rooz

Haft Seen - haft-seen

Sabzeh - sab-zay

Seer - sear

Somaq - soo-magh

Serkeh - ser-kay

Sonbol - sown-bowl

Sekkeh - sek-kay

Shirini - sheer-een-ee

Divan-e Hafez - Dee-vah-nee Hah-fez

Aideh Shomah Mobarak - aid-eh show-mah mo-bah-rack

Aide - aid-ee

Sabzi Polo Mahi - sabzee poe-low ma-hee

Kookoo Sabzi - kookoo sabzee

Seezdeh Bedar - seez-deh beh-dar

If I were to say to you, "Happy New Year!" what picture would come to your mind?

Would you picture a short, cold winter day?
Would everyone be staying up until midnight to shout
their greetings? Blowing horns and wearing party hats?

Well, I want you to picture something else…

Picture a day where the trees have buds, the first flowers are in bloom, and the days are getting longer. I want you to picture the first day of spring!

In a country called Iran, far across the world, people celebrate the New Year on the first day of spring, when everything starts anew. The trees will grow new leaves, the flowers new petals, and the grass new greenery. They call this day "Norooz," or "New Day." Persian people have celebrated this day for at least three thousand years.

Throughout those thousands of years, as people from the region journeyed to other countries, they brought the wonderful tradition of Norooz with them. Now, people living in places across the globe celebrate this day! From California, USA to Kabul, Afghanistan! From Sydney, Australia to Paris, France! They celebrate the first day of spring!

Let's take a look at how the festivities begin…

Preparations for the celebration begin well in advance. During the month before Norooz families spend their time baking pastries, cleaning (perhaps even painting) their homes, cleaning carpets, and rearranging the furniture. Everything should look fresh, clean and new for the first day of spring.

Not only should the house look as good as new, the people should look fresh, too! Everyone is busy shopping for new outfits to wear for the Norooz party!

The grocery stores are busy with people shopping for everything they will need in order to prepare their Norooz feasts. Fresh fish, vegetables, herbs and spices make for an amazing meal! Don't forget the flowers to decorate the tables, and fruits, tea and sweets to serve the many guests that will visit during the holiday season.

A very exciting day for everyone is the Wednesday evening before Norooz, called "Chahar Shanbeh Soori." This is when the real celebrations begin! On this night, all the families gather together. They build small bonfires in the street. Everyone runs and jumps over the fire, chanting, "Sorkhi-e toe az man, zardi-e man az toe!" or "Give me your vibrant (red) color and take my pale (yellow) color away!" In other words, on to the new and fresh!

People go through the streets banging on pots and pans with spoons, knocking on doors and asking for treats. This is called "Qashohg-Zany," or "spoon beating." They are clearing the way for good luck in the New Year!

On the streets you may see a man dressed in red satin, dancing and singing songs. This is Haji Firouz! He travels with his troubadours playing tambourines, kettle drums and trumpets. Hearing him on the streets fills everyone with excitement because it means Norooz is just around the corner!

In the house, everyone will set up a special table called the "Haft Seen," or the "Seven S" table. The Haft Seen will have seven items that begin with the sound "S." The table will have…

Serkeh – vinegar, representing age and patience.

Sabzeh – wheat or lentils grown in a tray or dish, representing rebirth.

Sonbol – the hyacinth flower with its strong fragrance announcing the coming of spring.

Sumac – representing the color of the sunrise.

Seeb – apple, representing beauty and health.

Seer – garlic, representing medicine.

Sekkeh – coins, representing prosperity and wealth.

Some other items on the table may include:

A Mirror – This is a symbol of light and eternity. It reflects back the goodness of the Haft Seen, and in a way, echoes it.

Goldfish – They symbolize life and the end of the Pisces zodiac sign.

A book of Divan-e Hafez – This is a book of famous Persian poetry.

Rosewater – It is thought to have magical cleansing powers.

Shirini – This is the Persian word for sugar cookies and pastries.

Candles – They symbolize enlightenment and happiness.

A copy of a holy book – This is to bless the New Year.

A Tangerine sitting in a bowl of water – It symbolizes the Earth floating in space.

Painted eggs – They symbolize new life.

Finally, the New Year approaches! When winter turns to spring and the Norooz begins, whether it is 3 in the morning or 3 in the afternoon, the family gathers around the Haft Seen table. At the exact moment when the sun crosses the equator, signaling the beginning of spring, they wish each other, "Aideh Shomah Mobarak!" or "Happy New Year!"

The children receive "Aide," a gift of new paper money or shiny coins, from all the adult relatives. Hugs, kisses, sweets and pastries for everyone!

They will share a special New Year's meal of "Sabzi Polo Mahi," or fish and rice with herbs, and "Kookoo Sabzi." Kookoo Sabzi is a delicious dish, similar to quiche, made with various greens, herbs and eggs.

For the next twelve days, when schools and many business are closed, they will spend their time visiting their families and friends – and their families and friends will visit them!

On the thirteenth day, called "Seezdeh Bedar," or "going out on the thirteenth," everyone heads outdoors for a picnic. This is the last day of the New Year holiday. It is a day to relax and enjoy time with family and friends in the new spring weather. Tomorrow, it's back to school and work.

At the end of the picnic, people take the Sabzeh they had grown in their homes and throw it in a river or stream. It has been growing in their house collecting all the bad energy from the old year, and now it is time to send it on its way!

So now, when you are smelling those first blossoms or enjoying the warmer weather on the first day of spring, remember that somewhere there are people welcoming and celebrating the spring in a most special way! Here's to your fresh start! May the pale days of the winter make way for the brighter days of the new spring, the New Year!

Aideh Shomah Mobarak everyone!

نوروز مبارک

Beyond the book...

Visit our webpage for information and ideas beyond the book!
www.no-rooz.com

For example:
Have you ever read your horoscope? The Persian months correspond with the dates of the astrological signs, or horoscopes. Visit our site to find out the date of your Persian birthday!

In our year 2016, Iran welcomed in the year 1395!

Many Iranians refer to the Los Angeles area as Tehrangeles (Tay-ron-gel-es) because it boasts the highest population of Iranians living outside Iran. Go to our site to see pictures of many of the wonderful stores and restaurants you can visit if you travel there!

Norooz is a non-religious holiday that originated in Iran (Persia), but because of the migration of Persians throughout history, it is also celebrated by people from many other areas, including Afghanistan, Eastern Turkey and Kazakhstan. Find a map highlighting all the areas of the world that celebrate Norooz at our webpage!

Print out Norooz coloring pages – Sonbol, Sabzeh, Seer!

Make the connection! Which parts of the Norooz celebration are celebrated in your culture?

Find directions for germinating your own Sabzeh.

www.no-rooz.com

About the Author: Gail Hejazi is a teacher in Princeton, New Jersey where she lives with her husband, daughter and son. She was inspired to write this book when her daughter was in kindergarten and the teacher invited parents to come in and share their holiday traditions with the class.

About the Illustrator: As well as being a talented artist, Chrissy Cavallo is also a fourth grade assistant teacher living in Hamilton, New Jersey. Chrissy has always been passionate about children's literature and she is excited to share this book with the world to teach people about Norooz.

Made in the USA
Las Vegas, NV
16 March 2025

19646891R00031